THE
Nativity
Coloring Book for Kids

This book belongs to:

ANNA
anna s. luce

Thank you so much for choosing
THE NATIVITY
COLORING BOOK
for kids ages 2+

Help your toddler discover the true meaning of Christmas by coloring <u>40 SIMPLE and BIG Christian illustrations based on the Nativity Story of Jesus!</u>

The large & easy designs will help your child learn about well-known Christian symbols and characters specific to the religious story of the birth of Jesus, such as: Mary, Joseph, Baby Jesus, Three Wise Men, the shepherds, the Bethlehem star, the angels, the manger, and many more!

Each illustration also includes an explanation, written in hollow letters for easy coloring. As your child colors, help him/her learn the story and understand the meaning of each symbol or scene in a friendly and playful way.

Did you like our book? Please <u>consider dropping us a review</u>. It takes only a few seconds and it really helps small businesses like ours reach more readers. Your support means the world to us.

Check out other books by Anna S. Luce on Amazon. Head over to our website <u>https://thelilabear.com</u> for more books, freebies and fun blog articles.

MARY

JOSEPH

ANGEL GABRIEL AND
THE ANNUNCIATION

MARY TRAVELS TO BETHLEHEM ON A DONKEY

ARIVING TO BETHLEHEM

THE STAR OF
BETHLEHEM

SHEEP
IN STABLE

OX
IN STABLE

LANTERN

STRAW CRADLE

BABY JESUS
IS BORN

BABY JESUS IN MANGER

HOLY FAMILY

SWADLING
CLOTHES

MARY WITH
BABY JESUS

THE LILY

HOLY BABY

JOSEPH WITH BABY JESUS

ANGEL SINGING
PRAISES TO GOD

THE THREE MAGI
SEE THE STAR

THE THREE WISE MEN COME TO BETHLEHEM

THEY TRAVEL
WITH CAMELS

PALM TREE

THEY BRING GIFTS
TO THE HOLY FAMILY

A GIFT FOR JESUS: GOLD

A GIFT FOR JESUS: FRANKINCENSE

A GIFT FOR JESUS:
MYRRH

SACRED HEART
OF JESUS

MARY
WITH BABY JESUS

WISEMAN'S CROWN

CANDLE

PRAYER
TO GOD

ANGEL

PEACE DOVE

I LOVE JESUS

ABC OF THE NATIVITY STORY

A is for ANGEL

B is for BETHLEHEM

C is for CRADLE

D is for DONKEY

E is for EMMANUEL

F is for FRANKINCENSE

G is for GOLD

H is for HOLY

I is for INCARNATION

J is for JESUS

K is for KING

L is for LAMB

M is for MARY

N is for NATIVITY

ABC OF THE NATIVITY STORY

O is for OX

P is for PALM TREE

Q is for QUIRINIUS*

R is for REJOICE

S is for STAR

T is for THREE WISE MEN

U is for UNITY

V is for VIRGIN MARY

W is for WORSHIP

X is for "X"MAS

Y is for YULE**

Z is for ZION

* the governor at the time of the census
**an old English word that refers to the winter season and the Christmas holiday

The Nativity Coloring Book for Kids

Made in the USA
Columbia, SC
08 December 2024

48757216R00048